EDGE BOOKS

Ghosts of the ALAMO

AND OTHER HAUNTINGS OF THE SOUTH

by Matt Chandler

Edge Books are published by Capstone Press,
1710 Roe Crest Drive, North Mankato, Minnesota 56003
www.capstonepub.com

Library of Congress Cataloging-in-Publication Data
Chandler, Matt.
  Ghosts of the Alamo and other hauntings of the South / by Matt Chandler.
    pages cm—(Edge Books: Haunted America)
  Includes index and bibliographical references.
  Summary: "Describes ghost sightings and hauntings in the southern United
States"—Provided by publisher.
  ISBN 978-1-4765-3914-0 (library binding)
  ISBN 978-1-4765-5962-9 (eBook PDF)
1. Haunted places—Southern States—Juvenile literature. 2. Ghosts—Southern
States—Juvenile literature. I. Title.
  BF1472.U6C43 2014
  133.10975—dc23   2013031836

Editorial Credits
Anthony Wacholtz, editor; Heidi Thompson, designer; Marcie Spence,
media researcher; Danielle Ceminsky, production specialist

Photo Credits
Benjamin Jeffries, 16–17; Capstone: 13 (bottom), 14; Getty Images: Flickr Vision/
Steven Wagner, 10–11, Lonely Planet Images/Stephen Saks, 8–9, Visions of America,
20–21; Janice and Nolan Braud: 22–23, Mammoth Cave National Park Service: 18–19;
Newscom: Mark Washburn/MCT, 24–25, 26–27; Shutterstock: Dmitry Natashin,
design element, echo3005, design element, gracious_tiger, 5, Jorg Hackemann, 4,
nikkytok, design element, urbanlight, 7; Wayne Hsieh, 12–13, 15e

Direct Quotations
Page 7: Mary Beth Crain. *Haunted U.S. Battlefields*. Connecticut: Globe Pequot Press,
2008, 128–129.
Page 15: Troy Taylor. *The Haunting of America*. New York: Fall River Press, 2006, 224.
Page 23: Ibid., 176.
Page 26: Joanne Austin. *Weird Encounters*. New York: Sterling Publishing, 2010, 295.

Printed in the United States of America.
032017   010318R

TABLE OF CONTENTS

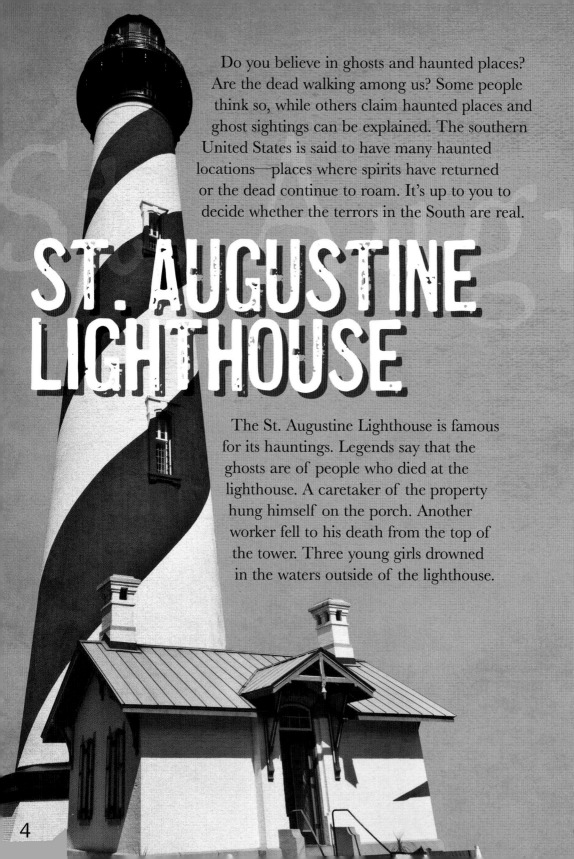

Do you believe in ghosts and haunted places? Are the dead walking among us? Some people think so, while others claim haunted places and ghost sightings can be explained. The southern United States is said to have many haunted locations—places where spirits have returned or the dead continue to roam. It's up to you to decide whether the terrors in the South are real.

ST. AUGUSTINE LIGHTHOUSE

The St. Augustine Lighthouse is famous for its hauntings. Legends say that the ghosts are of people who died at the lighthouse. A caretaker of the property hung himself on the porch. Another worker fell to his death from the top of the tower. Three young girls drowned in the waters outside of the lighthouse.

Today people claim to have experienced ghostly events at the lighthouse. The laughter of young girls can be heard when no children are there. A ghost that looks like the man who fell is said to roam the property. Some reports involve the **spirit** of the caretaker. He was known to enjoy smoking cigars while on duty. Visitors have smelled fresh cigar smoke on the property, even though no one is smoking nearby.

the spiral staircase of the St. Augustine Lighthouse

spirit—another name for a ghost

THE ALAMO

In 1836 a 13-day battle took place at the Alamo in San Antonio, Texas. Between 800 and 2,000 men were killed in the bloody conflict between Texan fighters and the Mexican army. More than 175 years later, people claim the spirits of the dead roam free at the historic Texas landmark.

The Alamo was originally built in the 1700s as Mission San Antonio de Valero. It was supposed to be a place of worship and religious education. Instead, it became a landmark for the famous standoff. The historic location is open for tours today.

Sightings of the fighters' spirits are commonly reported at the Alamo. A visitor heard voices echoing in one building, yet he knew he was alone. The voices got louder and louder. Finally, one voice called out to the man, "It's too late!" The man left the building and went straight to the Alamo security.

A worker at the Alamo has heard spirits call out. The spirits seem to be carrying out the famous battle. The worker claims to have heard "Fire!" "He's dead!" and "Here they come!" from within the Alamo.

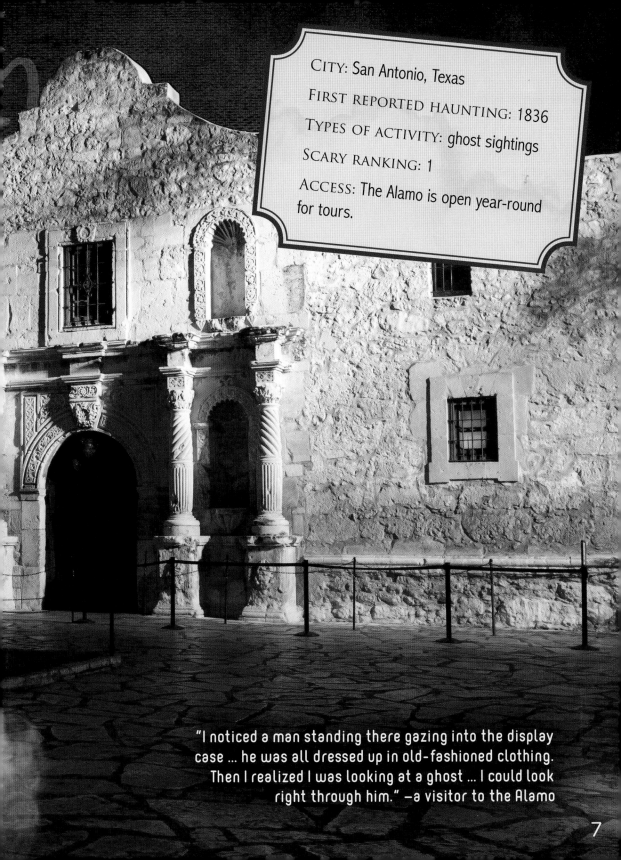

CITY: San Antonio, Texas

FIRST REPORTED HAUNTING: 1836

TYPES OF ACTIVITY: ghost sightings

SCARY RANKING: 1

ACCESS: The Alamo is open year-round for tours.

"I noticed a man standing there gazing into the display case ... he was all dressed up in old-fashioned clothing. Then I realized I was looking at a ghost ... I could look right through him." —a visitor to the Alamo

MYRTLES PLANTATION

Myrtles Plantation was built more than 200 years ago. Today the plantation is a bed and breakfast, restaurant, and the site of various receptions. But it is also considered one of the most haunted houses in America. Many people have owned the home, and each owner has experienced **paranormal** activity.

The most famous ghost is Chloe, a young slave who was killed on the property. Legend says she poisoned members of the family who lived there. She was hung, and her body was thrown into a river. Visitors to the plantation have claimed to see Chloe in guest rooms and on the grounds. Chloe was missing an ear. Witnesses report seeing Chloe's ghost wearing a green scarf to cover the missing ear. It is said that Chloe steals earrings from guest rooms and pins them on the scarf.

According to visitors, Chloe isn't the only ghost at the plantation. Crying babies are heard when none are in the building. Footsteps echo down empty hallways. **Apparitions** wander in the lobby. Many guests are so terrified they leave in the middle of the night.

CITY: near St. Francisville, Louisiana

FIRST REPORTED HAUNTING: 1950s

TYPES OF ACTIVITY: vanishing objects, strange smells, unexplained footsteps

SCARY RANKING: 2

ACCESS: Tours are offered.

paranormal—having to do with an unexplained event
apparition—the visible appearance of a ghost

THE LALAURIE MANSION

New Orleans is a popular vacation spot for tourists, attracting millions of visitors each year. But visitors may not know the legendary paranormal history of the bustling city. In the center is the LaLaurie Mansion, also known as Hell House. Delphine LaLaurie lived in the mansion and was known to abuse her slaves. She once chased a young slave across the roof of the home with a whip. The girl jumped to her death and was buried on the property.

CITY: New Orleans, Louisiana

FIRST REPORTED HAUNTING: 1834

TYPES OF ACTIVITY: ghostly screams, unexplained noises

SCARY RANKING: 4

ACCESS: The mansion is privately owned and not open for tours.

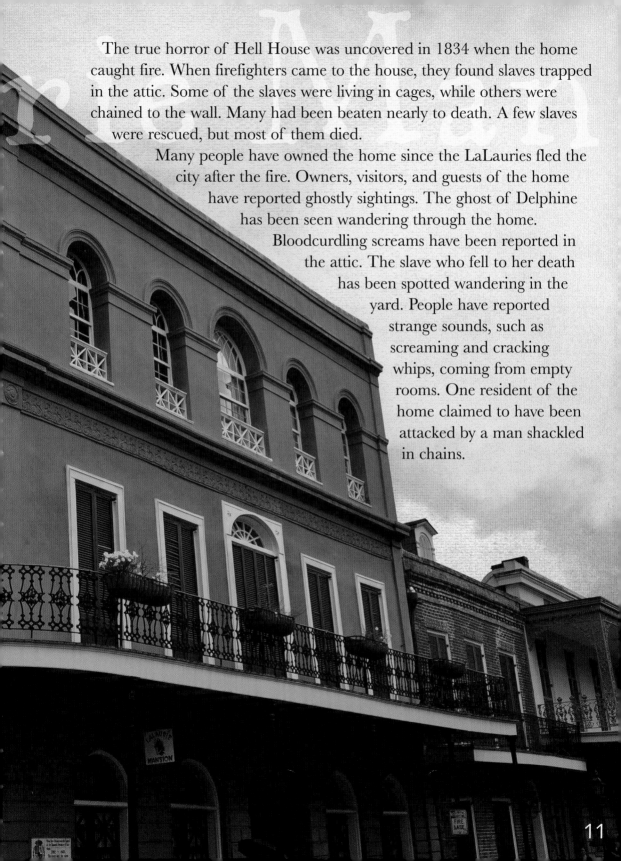

The true horror of Hell House was uncovered in 1834 when the home caught fire. When firefighters came to the house, they found slaves trapped in the attic. Some of the slaves were living in cages, while others were chained to the wall. Many had been beaten nearly to death. A few slaves were rescued, but most of them died.

Many people have owned the home since the LaLauries fled the city after the fire. Owners, visitors, and guests of the home have reported ghostly sightings. The ghost of Delphine has been seen wandering through the home. Bloodcurdling screams have been reported in the attic. The slave who fell to her death has been spotted wandering in the yard. People have reported strange sounds, such as screaming and cracking whips, coming from empty rooms. One resident of the home claimed to have been attacked by a man shackled in chains.

BELL WITCH CAVE

The Bell Witch Cave in Tennessee was named after a spirit that supposedly haunted the area. But the hauntings didn't begin in the cave. Starting in 1817, John Bell and his family were haunted by a ghost that became known as the Bell Witch of Tennessee. Bell was a wealthy farmer who owned a great deal of land. The property was where the witch terrorized the Bell family and anyone who visited the farm.

CITY: Adams, Tennessee

FIRST REPORTED HAUNTING: 1817

TYPES OF ACTIVITY: strange noises, apparitions, unexplained death

SCARY RANKING: 5

ACCESS: Public tours of the cave and the property are available.

The haunting of Bell Farm became well known because of the Bell Witch's reported aggressive behavior. The witch was believed to be responsible for injuring several members of the family. The family heard strange noises and knocks at the door when no one was there. Scratching and clawing sounds were heard at night with no explanation. Then the children began to be attacked while they slept. Their hair was violently pulled, and their covers were ripped from their beds. Yet when they awoke, they were alone.

the home of John Bell

The Bell Witch is said to have communicated with family members and visitors to the farm. Many people reported speaking directly with the witch. She seemed to be very angry with the family, especially John Bell. "I'll keep after him until the end of his days!" the witch reportedly told visitors to the Bell Farm. "Old Jack Bell's days are numbered." According to legend, the witch kept her promise. She was blamed for murdering John Bell by poisoning him while he slept.

Today the home is no longer standing on the property. However, visitors can take a tour of the Bell Witch Cave and the land where the Bell Witch terrorized the family. Tourists have reported strange and unexplained occurrences in the cave. One woman claimed to see the ghost of a woman floating across the cave entrance.

After John died, his family found a vial of fluid. They realized John had been poisoned after giving some of the fluid to the cat, which died.

"It had the complete figure of a person [until] it got down to about its ankles. It wasn't touching the floor at all. It was just drifting ... bouncing along."
– Bill Eden, former owner of the land describing a ghost he saw

15

WAVERLY HILLS SANATORIUM

The original Waverly Hills **Sanatorium** was built in 1910, but it was remodeled from 1924 to 1926 and reopened. The new building was used as a hospital for people suffering from the deadly disease **tuberculosis**. But what was supposed to be a place for medical treatment soon became a terrifying location.

Thousands of patients died at Waverly. The facility had a 500-foot (152-meter) tunnel used to carry supplies in and out of the sanatorium. Eventually, the dead were transported to the bottom of the property through the tunnel. It became known as the "body chute" or "death tunnel," and it was the scene of many ghostly occurrences.

CITY: Louisville, Kentucky

FIRST REPORTED HAUNTING: 1962

TYPES OF ACTIVITY: Unexplained noises, ghostly sightings

SCARY RANKING: 4

ACCESS: Tours are available, including private overnight tours.

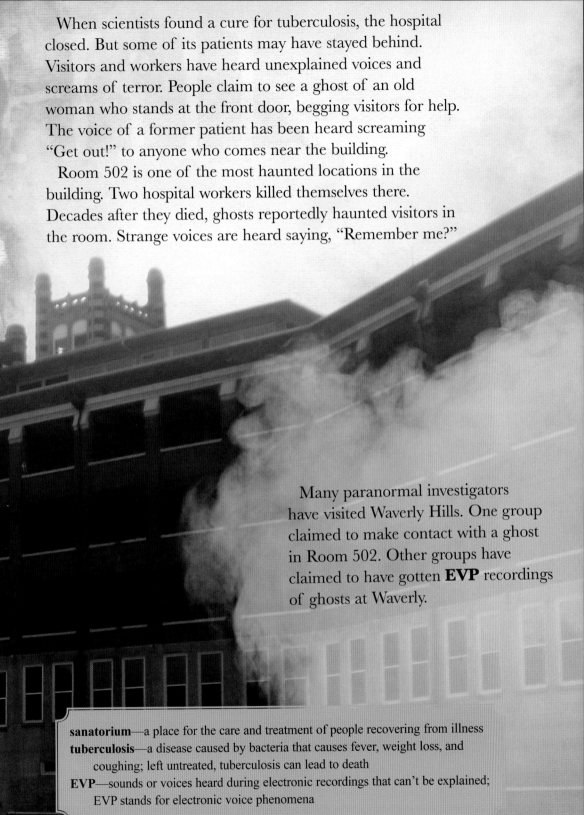

When scientists found a cure for tuberculosis, the hospital closed. But some of its patients may have stayed behind. Visitors and workers have heard unexplained voices and screams of terror. People claim to see a ghost of an old woman who stands at the front door, begging visitors for help. The voice of a former patient has been heard screaming "Get out!" to anyone who comes near the building.

Room 502 is one of the most haunted locations in the building. Two hospital workers killed themselves there. Decades after they died, ghosts reportedly haunted visitors in the room. Strange voices are heard saying, "Remember me?"

Many paranormal investigators have visited Waverly Hills. One group claimed to make contact with a ghost in Room 502. Other groups have claimed to have gotten **EVP** recordings of ghosts at Waverly.

sanatorium—a place for the care and treatment of people recovering from illness
tuberculosis—a disease caused by bacteria that causes fever, weight loss, and coughing; left untreated, tuberculosis can lead to death
EVP—sounds or voices heard during electronic recordings that can't be explained; EVP stands for electronic voice phenomena

MAMMOTH CAVE

The Mammoth Cave in Kentucky is the largest known cave system in the world. It is also considered to be one of the most haunted caves in the world. Settlers originally explored the cave searching for valuable minerals. Mining is dangerous work, and many settlers were killed. Some of the bodies remained in the cave for many years.

Today the cave is part of a national park. Visitors take tours of the cave. Many have reported having paranormal experiences. There have been sightings of ghostly apparitions in the cave. Some of the scariest moments come when the tour guides conduct a "blackout." During a blackout, they turn off the lights. One park guide claimed to have been shoved and heard footsteps when no one was around.

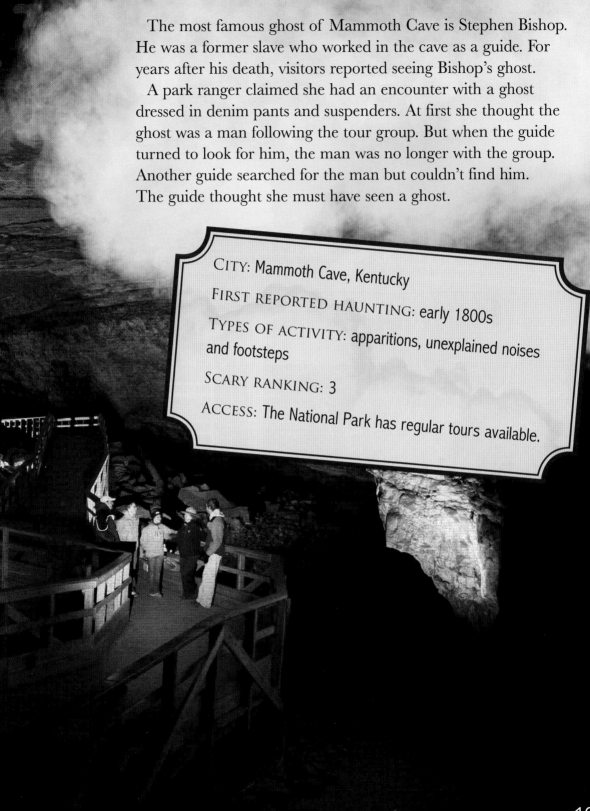

The most famous ghost of Mammoth Cave is Stephen Bishop. He was a former slave who worked in the cave as a guide. For years after his death, visitors reported seeing Bishop's ghost.

A park ranger claimed she had an encounter with a ghost dressed in denim pants and suspenders. At first she thought the ghost was a man following the tour group. But when the guide turned to look for him, the man was no longer with the group. Another guide searched for the man but couldn't find him. The guide thought she must have seen a ghost.

CITY: Mammoth Cave, Kentucky

FIRST REPORTED HAUNTING: early 1800s

TYPES OF ACTIVITY: apparitions, unexplained noises and footsteps

SCARY RANKING: 3

ACCESS: The National Park has regular tours available.

THE BILTMORE HOTEL

The Biltmore Hotel in Florida is a place where the rich and famous used to stay. It is also a place where one **infamous** guest met his end.

Gangster Thomas "Fats" Walsh ran an illegal gambling operation from a suite on the 13th floor. One night in 1929, an angry gambler shot Fats, and the famous gangster died in the bathroom. His blood left a permanent stain on the marble of the bathroom floor.

Walsh's ghost is said to be very active at the hotel. Guests say the elevator skips stops and takes them directly to the 13th floor. When the doors open, Walsh can be heard shouting and screaming.

CITY: Coral Gables, Florida

FIRST REPORTED HAUNTING: 1960s

TYPES OF ACTIVITY: ghosts, unexplained noises, objects moving

SCARY RANKING: 5

ACCESS: The hotel is still in operation.

Witnesses have reported seeing many other ghosts at the Biltmore. Most of the ghosts are said to be friendly. A dishwasher claimed he saw the ghost of a man dressed in a top hat playing the piano. He might have been playing music for the ghostly couples sometimes spotted in the ballroom dancing. Witnesses say they were dressed in old-fashioned clothing and were **transparent**. Another ghost is said to appear on the 13th floor of the Biltmore. One guest said the ghost greeted her and was very friendly.

infamous—known for a negative act or behavior
transparent—easily seen through

21

THE CRESCENT HOTEL

The Crescent Hotel seemed doomed to be haunted before the first guest arrived. While the hotel was being built in 1884, a worker fell through the roof and died. His body landed where room 218 of the hotel is located today. One guest of room 218 reported waking in the middle of the night being violently shaken. He heard footsteps moving across the room but saw no one. Another guest in the room woke one night to see the walls spattered with blood. She is said to have run from the room screaming. When hotel workers investigated, the walls looked normal.

In the 1930s Norman Baker bought the hotel to open a hospital. According to legend, Baker did experiments on his patients, killing many of them. He eventually went to prison for mail fraud. More than 70 years later, guests have claimed to see the ghost of Baker wandering the halls of the hotel.

The hotel is once again open for guests, and the paranormal reports continue to roll in. Witnesses say a ghost wanders the lobby dressed in formal clothing of the Victorian Era. He never speaks and never bothers anyone. Guests also report doors slamming and other ghost sightings. One of the most terrifying accounts happened when a family in room 424 was watching TV. Suddenly an apparition walked through the closed and locked door. It wandered across the room and into the bathroom. The terrified family fled the Crescent and never returned.

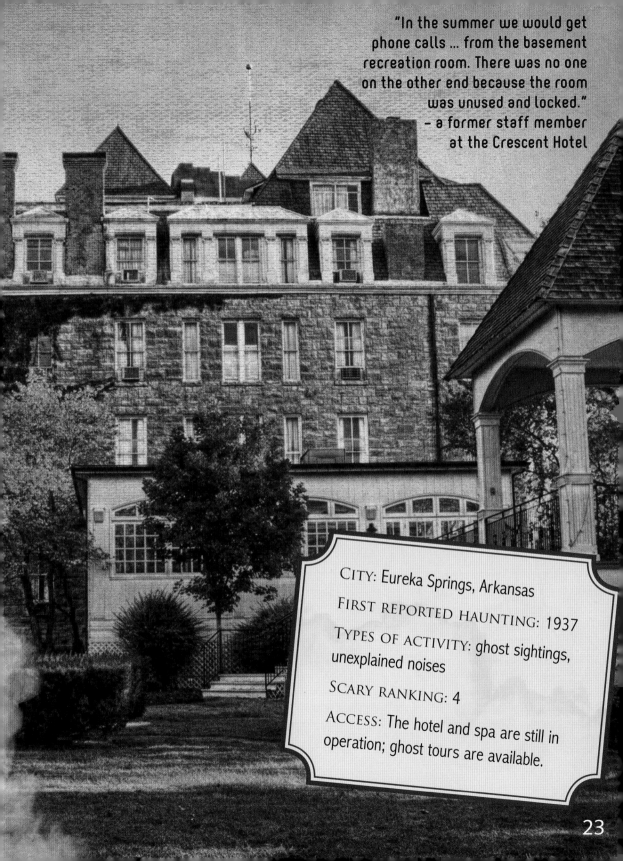

"In the summer we would get phone calls ... from the basement recreation room. There was no one on the other end because the room was unused and locked."
– a former staff member at the Crescent Hotel

CITY: Eureka Springs, Arkansas

FIRST REPORTED HAUNTING: 1937

TYPES OF ACTIVITY: ghost sightings, unexplained noises

SCARY RANKING: 4

ACCESS: The hotel and spa are still in operation; ghost tours are available.

MOUNDSVILLE PENITENTIARY

Moundsville Penitentiary in West Virginia was shut down in 1995. But for more than 100 years, it held some of the most violent prisoners in the country. More than 1,000 men died inside the walls of Moundsville. Many were hung or electrocuted for their crimes. Others were beaten to death in prison riots. Some died in fights between inmates living in horrible, overcrowded conditions.

Guards, inmates, and visitors have reported strange events at the prison since the 1930s. Unexplained noises, freezing cold spots in the middle of summer, and ghostly apparitions are part of the prison **lore**.

One of the most infamous murders in the prison occurred in 1929. R.D. Wall was an inmate at Moundsville. Three new inmates saw him talking to guards one day. The inmates later cornered Wall and brutally attacked him. Since then there have been many sightings of a ghost—possibly Wall—wandering the maintenance area of the prison.

CITY: Moundsville, West Virginia

FIRST REPORTED HAUNTING: as early as the 1930s; many reports began in the 1990s after the prison was closed

TYPES OF ACTIVITY: ghost sightings, unexplained voices, footsteps, and screams

SCARY RANKING: 3

ACCESS: Guided tours are available, including overnight stays.

lore—a collection of knowledge and traditions of a particular group that has been passed down over generations

One of the scariest reports involves a headless ghost seen wandering the halls. Many people think the ghost is Frank Hyer, an inmate who was hanged at Moundsville in 1931. He was the last of 94 prisoners who were executed at the penitentiary.

The prison is open for tours, and brave souls can even spend the night in one of the cells. Many people report hearing unexplained noises and feeling sudden cold chills. There are regular sightings of **orbs** and ghostly apparitions.

"There was something like a light bar moving around ... like it was walking back and forth, pacing at the top of the stairs, which led to the basement of the penitentiary."
— a tour worker at Moundsville

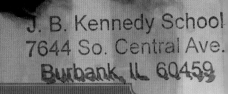

Hauntings: Fact or Fiction?

Do the spirits of the dead haunt the hotels, houses, and other buildings of the South? Or are there logical explanations behind the encounters? Whether you're a believer or a **skeptic**, you may want to leave the lights on if you visit these places!

orb—a glowing ball of light that sometimes appears in photographs taken at reportedly haunted locations

skeptic—a person who questions things that other people believe in

HAUNTED PLACES IN THIS BOOK

Moundsville Penitentiary

Waverly Hills Sanatorium

Mammoth Cave

Bell Witch Cave

The Crescent Hotel

Myrtles Plantation

St. Augustine Lighthouse

The Alamo

The LaLaurie Mansion

The Biltmore Hotel

OTHER HAUNTED LOCATIONS OF THE SOUTH

- Eliza Thompson House in Savannah, Georgia
- King's Tavern in Natchez, Mississippi
- Hammock House in Beaufort, North Carolina
- Menger Hotel in San Antonio, Texas
- Cedar Grove Inn in Vicksburg, Mississippi
- Catfish Plantation Restaurant in Waxahachie, Texas
- Jameson Inn in Crestview, Florida
- Kehoe House in Savannah, Georgia
- Sweetwater Mansion in Florence, Alabama
- Magnolia Manor in Bolivar, Tennessee
- Old Charleston Jail in Charleston, South Carolina
- Peavey Melody Music in Meridian, Mississippi

GLOSSARY

apparition (ap-uh-RISH-uhn)—the visible appearance of a ghost

EVP—sounds or voices heard during electronic recordings that can't be explained; EVP stands for electronic voice phenomenon

infamous (IN-fuh-muhss)—known for a negative act or behavior

lore (LORE)—a collection of knowledge and traditions of a particular group that has been passed down over generations

orb (AWRB)—a glowing ball of light that sometimes appears in photographs taken at reportedly haunted locations

paranormal (pair-uh-NOR-muhl)—having to do with an unexplained event that has no scientific explanation

plantation (plan-TAY-shuhn)—a large farm where crops such as cotton and sugarcane are grown

sanatorium (san-uh-TOR-i-uhm)—a place for the care and treatment of people recovering from illness

skeptic (SKEP-tik)—a person who questions things that other people believe in

spirit (SPIHR-it)—another name for a ghost

transparent (transs-PAIR-uhnt)—easily seen through

tuberculosis (tu-BUR-kyoo-low-sis)—a disease caused by bacteria that causes fever, weight loss, and coughing; left untreated, tuberculosis can lead to death

READ MORE

Belanger, Jeff. *The World's Most Haunted Places.* Haunted: Ghosts and the Paranormal. New York: Rosen Publishing, 2009.

Chandler, Matt. *The World's Most Haunted Places.* The Ghost Files. Mankato, Minn.: Capstone Press. 2012.

Everett, J. H., and Marilyn Scott-Waters. *Haunted Histories: Creepy Castles, Dark Dungeons, and Powerful Palaces.* New York: Henry Holt and Company, 2012.

INTERNET SITES

FactHound offers a safe, fun way to find Internet sites related to this book. All of the sites on FactHound have been researched by our staff.

Here's all you do:

Visit *www.facthound.com*

Type in this code: 9781476539140

Check out projects, games and lots more at
www.capstonekids.com

INDEX